Dear Jenny

Nerelle Poroch

Dear Jenny

Dear Jenny
ISBN 978 1 76041 370 5
Copyright © text Nerelle Poroch 2017
Cover photo by Jenny's family, 2015

First published 2017 by
GINNINDERRA PRESS
PO Box 3461 Port Adelaide 5015
www.ginninderrapress.com.au

This is a story of love between two women, Jenny and Nerelle, who shared many years of friendship. Their expressions of love through phone texts from June to September 2015 gradually became less self-conscious as death approached following Jenny's diagnosis of cancer.

I met Jenny on my first day in the Property Directorate of the Commonwealth Public Service. She and I were the only females in an all-male branch. We maintained government buildings, planned the location of public servants in various areas of Canberra and acquired leases to house them in privately owned buildings. It was the early 70s, and the time before the 'women's libbers' moved into this area of work and occupied managerial positions. They put a stop to the fellows reading girlie magazines hidden in the paper files. When they overstayed lunch at the club, their female managers made a habit of entering the club to present them with leave forms to cover the extra time spent there. Like many women of our era, we had previously turned a blind eye to all of this and diligently carried out our work.

So our friendship grew. We were like-minded about work, serious about the job, but did not take ourselves too seriously. Although in later years we worked in different sections of the Property Directorate, our friendship was maintained. Jenny was a fiercely serious and confident employee. When Jenny worked in the minister's office, I was in awe of her abilities. She respected mine and one year I was told that she had submitted my name for the annual Public Service Medal.

Jenny and I shared interests in real estate, thriller novels, the soap *The Bold and the Beautiful*, movies, Radio National, politics, and just being alive. We laughed a lot when together. In humour we shared the ironies of life and our similar experiences growing up.

So Jenny retired and revelled in this time of her life. She had been a single mother for a long time and now it was time for her to relax a little and enjoy having coffee, meeting friends, reading books and visiting her grandchildren.

Jenny is the only person in the world who habitually popped in to see me unannounced, whether we lived in adjoining suburbs or in the next street. I did the same with her. It was a lovely catch-up thing we did. We laughed a lot and discussed our concerns of the time during these visits and met regularly for dinner at our favourite restaurant. On one such occasion early in 2015 she was significantly thinner. I wondered at her ability to loose weight and was on the verge of asking about a special diet she might have found. But I didn't.

In February 2015 she popped in and said she had inoperable cancer. Over a cup of tea we talked about her devastation on receiving such news. But she would face this bravely as she had done other tragedies in her life. Jenny wanted to be alive to see the birth of a grandchild, the biological child of her daughter Naomi and husband Matt carried to birth by their friend. And she was able to see her granddaughter Lucy born in April 2015.

By June the chemotherapy was too harsh for her tiny, wasted body and she decided not to continue with any treatment. So I was the only one popping in. Her two daughters and her sister and son cared for Jenny at home and when the time came for me to leave for six weeks in Italy and Russia, I said goodbye with a heavy heart. At the door saying our goodbyes, Jenny dreamed of the possibility that we could have seen Italy together.

So I decided to take Jenny with me on my journey to Italy and Russia. She accompanied me through the flow of texts we exchanged during part of her brave journey through cancer. The strength of our friendship is revealed through these regular texts and our frequent communication after I returned, up until Jenny's death in September 2015.

Others in this story are my pregnant Russian teacher Anna, married to Paolo living in Genoa; Evgueny, my Russian teacher living in Saint Petersburg; and Antonina, my friend with whom I have stayed in Petersburg over the last eight years. Important others in this journey are Jenny's sister Marilyn; daughters Rachel and Naomi, and her daughter Lucy; Jenny's son Ben; and husbands of her daughters, Duncan and Matt; her grandchildren; long-time friends Ella and Ian; and my partner, Philip.

At the end of her life, Jenny reached the point of readiness for death only when she had accomplished several things. They were Lucy's birth in April 2015, family togetherness and gatherings, and organising a gift for forty nurses at the hospice in appreciation for their wonderful care. Jenny's texts are briefer than mine, but show how she expressed her love for me and I for her. Gaps in Jenny's replies represent times when she was 'not feeling brilliant'.

Stopover in Dubai en route to Italy

Saturday 6 June 2015

– Hi Jenny. The adventure has begun. Just landed in Dubai, the Mecca of shopping. By the way it's 6 a.m. and I've left my watch in the security check. Oops. Have to see someone to get it back! N

Saturday 6 June 2015

– I'm wearing your top. It's great. Love you so much. Jenny.

Saturday 6 June 2015

– Dear Jenny, glad the top is great. Lucky I texted you and then found I didn't have my watch. The Information lady brought me back to security. They turned the baskets inside out and found it! Lucky another flight wasn't arriving. Then I left my new thriller I just bought there and I heard someone saying when I got off the escalator, 'Madame, here is your book.' Have to walk a few miles now to my gate of departure. N x

Saturday 6 June 2015

– Enjoy your trip. I'm thinking of you with admiration and envy :-) Jenny

Sunday 7 June 2015

– Dear Jenny, thinking of you as I look out of the train on way to Genoa. The countryside is green with lots of fields. It's 30 degrees here and the trip has been tiring, with a three-hour train journey on top from Milan. But I'm nearly, nearly there with the help of a few people at Milan station showing me how and where to buy the train ticket. I hope you're feeling a little stronger. Love, Nerelle

Sunday 7 June 2015

– Dear Jenny, it's probably the middle of the night for you. How are you? I hope you had a good day. Getting my bearings. My friend located me next to a big shopping centre. They bring dogs into the centre and the dogs stroll through with owners. Weather 26 degrees. I have Italian translation on my mobile, which helps. You really saved me from loosing my watch in Dubai. As I was texting you, I looked for the time and it wasn't there. All for now. N xx

Monday 8 June 2015

– So lovely to get your interesting messages, Nerelle. I feel like you're still here. Went for a drive to Captains Flat yesterday. Really enjoyed it. Bit different from Italy, though! Sounds like you're having a great time. Love you and am so proud of you. Jenny

Monday 8 June 2015

– Dear Jenny, lovely to receive your news. So glad you enjoyed Captains Flat. Remember when Ella lived there? I haven't been there for a long time. Wayne McGregor lived there as well, I think, for a while. Now there's a name from the past.

I visited Anna and Paolo yesterday. I can walk there. They live on the top floor and one has to go up 100-plus steps. As it's hot, Anna can only go out once a day as the steps are too many at the moment for a pregnant lady. She is well. The baby is a girl. They're thinking of a name like Alisha or Alena some Italian/Russian version of Alice. Up another flight is a large terrace. You would love it. In big tubs with a watering system is honeysuckle which grows up a pergola. The periphery of the large terrace contains tubs of different plants. I could send you photos on Naomi's phone if she has a smart phone or Ben's phone. I live in a district without tourists so my experience is very Italian. The hotel is located below people's apartments and is small. I could have been the only resident last night.

There are lots of African refugees here. I gather it's best not to walk around certain places. People from Bangladesh also live here. I'm told they work around the clock. The hotel receptionist is Bangladeshi. He only speaks a little English. I show him the Italian translation on the phone to converse. There are people in Genoa from Ecuador of all places. Paolo thinks the Catholic Church is bringing them here to balance up the Muslim refugees. What a problem. I think the book about the Muslim religion is probably raising lots of questions for you to think about.

I go to Anna for a three-hour Russian lesson this morning at 10 a.m. as it will be cool on the terrace. Anna's delighted to be able to speak Russian with me. She's learning Italian. Sometimes when she speaks English she speaks English, Italian and Russian in one sentence. Paolo speaks English but doesn't understand all. His work previously brought him to Singapore where he worked with an Australian-born colleague and an Australian who was born in the Philippines. He could only understand the latter, who had to then pass on the messages to the Australian-born colleague.

Time to get out of bed so I can remember how to find Anna's 100-plus-step apartment. Sleep well, dear Jenny. Love from Nerelle

PS Genoa is only eight hours behind. I thought it would be nearly evening in Canberra and just googled. It's only 14.30 in Canberra. N x

Wednesday 10 June 2015

– Dear Jenny, How are you? Hope you're feeling stronger. Sending you much love. Nerelle xx

Wednesday 10 June 2015

– Thanks for your lovely support. I'm feeling OK. Still enough energy to loathe Joe Hockey and his out-of-touch remarks on housing. What are you up to? Have lessons started? I really look forward to your messages. Thinking of you with lots of love.
Jenny

Wednesday 10 June 2015

– Dear Jenny, I'm in a café I visit every day on the way to Anna's house and lessons. The serving lady looks like a retired blonde prostitute wearing shorts and lips painted up to her nose! Music is playing in the foreground, and when I leave I'm farewelled with *ciao cara*. More later. N xx

Thursday 11 June 2015

– Keep those stories coming. Glad you're having a lovely time. Your traveller's tales are great. Love you and thinking of you.
Jenny

Thursday 11 June 2015

– Dear Jenny, here I am again at the café with all those who come every day. I don't have to order the cappuccino now. After three days, the lady I described knows me. Loud dancing music is playing. Old ladies stand at the bar drinking coffee and gossiping.

I'm glad you've been feeling OK and that Joe Hockey is stirring your better sense. My hotel is modest. The man from Bangladesh who manages it sleeps in a box room marked toilet. He's there around the clock.

I'm really enjoying the lessons with Anna. For the lessons, we go up yet another set of stairs to the terrace, sip water and dip into a bowl of cherries and debate so far about globalisation and immigration swamping Italy. Anna said a McDonalds started up in a small town in Italy and closed because the locals preferred Italian food. It's all about food here. Wonderful markets with fresh everything. I feel as if I've been here longer. Anna's very hospitable and makes me eat salads after the lesson. Paolo is painting his small boat, which Anna describes as a cup.

Oh my God, one of the lady owners of the café has just appeared in polka dot tights and a short, short skirt!

Today we're having lunch with Paolo's parents. They live in a small village not far away. Will be able to tell you about it next time. Keep strong and enjoy each day. Much love from me. N xxx

Forgot to add, the bar ladies have tattoos and the dogs who are coffee-housing with their owners today are fighting!

Thursday 11 June 2015

– Nerelle, keep copies of your messages. I reckon you could publish them. Terrific! Love you heaps. Jenny

Thursday 11 June 2015

– Dear Jenny, good suggestion. Glad you're enjoying them. N xx

Friday 12 June 2015

– Dear Jenny, I hope you're going along all right and are managing some trips out of the house. I'm in my coffee shop, which is really a bar but old and young come in. This time it's after my lesson, and unlike mornings when the streets are very busy, in the afternoons the shops close and reopen later. Therefore there's hardly a soul around. I've had lessons each day with Anna under her honeysuckle-covered bamboo pergola which Paolo made on their terrace. The 100-plus steps to her apartment are keeping me fit. After class today, Paolo made spaghetti. On other days, they insist that I eat a salad before I leave for home. I did buy presents of wine which we opened for dinner one night and then we spent many hours on the terrace under the pergola. I feel embarrassed at their hospitality. We had lunch at Paolo's parents' house yesterday. It's located on the seafront at a place called Pele, which is the birthplace of the architect Renzo Piano. He's presently building things at Barangaroo in Sydney on the harbour. During the weekend there are places on the coast to visit. Will write again soon. Much love to you from me.

Saturday 13 June 2015

– Do you eat at the coffee shop? What's the food like there? Love hearing from you. Jenny

Saturday 13 June 2015

– Dear Jenny, just had a cappuccino at the bar as have just finished breakfast at my simple hotel of cappuccino, toast and croissants in packets which they buy from supermarkets. I've had a lovely fresh salad which Anna has prepared of lettuce, radishes, tomatoes but they individually add oil and sea salt. Paolo has made spaghetti pasta – one with fish and another with herbs and very small dry fish. His mother, for lunch, prepared the Italian rice dish with beans and asparagus. Can't remember name but you'll remember. One reduces the water and the rice is lovely. After that, stuffed tomatoes, onions, zucchini with filling of egg, cheese, breadcrumbs. Then strawberry, bananas, ice cream and coffee in very small cups. I hope this description has built your appetite and you're now rushing to the kitchen to eat. Italians are all about eating from the fresh fruit and vegetable markets everywhere, and fish and pizza and cake shops. I'm even beginning to like the hotel breakfast. Will say goodbye for now. Thinking of you. With love from Nerelle

Saturday 13 June 2015

– Dear Jenny, sitting on a railway platform on way to small village. People from Africa begging in the streets. I feel I'm a good target. A bit scary and sad. I've reached Nervi, the village where rich people have their villas. Still exploring. N x

Saturday 13 June 2015

– You'll come back a little porker. Went to the pictures with Ben this morning. Saw latest Helen Mirren movie about art stolen by the Nazis. We took my hot water bottle for comfort. Have a lovely time away, Nerelle. Jenny :-)

Come home soon. Your traveller's tales will be so interesting. J

Sunday 14 June 2015

– Dear Jenny, so glad you enjoyed the movie. I saw the shorts. Helen Mirren plays an interesting role, I think. She can turn herself into so many different people. Yes, I'll have to eat salads most of the time and stay away from the gelato! Love, Nerelle

Monday 15 June 2015

– Dear Jenny, feel a bit homesick today. I'm on my way to lessons. Anna was a bit Soviet on Friday, meaning she ran out of patience with my slow, tired brain and I'm not too keen to repeat that today. My teachers, Amin in Canberra and Evgueny in Saint Petersburg, both realise I'm doing this for enjoyment but other Russian teachers have what I call a Soviet attitude. But visited a lovely place on the sparkling sea on Saturday. Went by train and it was only six stops away. I hope you get the chance to enjoy another visit to the movies and do other nice things. Love to you from me. N x

Monday 15 June 2015

– You're gorgeous and we're homesick for you too. I didn't send on to Phil the message you sent me by mistake as I didn't know how to! But I did think how cute you are. Ella came around today, which was lovely. When you feel homesick, do remember how much you're missed back here. And you're travelling for me too as well. I love your stories. Keep up the good work. Much love. Jenny

Tuesday 16 June 2015

– Dear Jenny, at the café on way to lesson and don't have to order cappuccino. They just prepare it. I've noticed these strange things: a dog in the big shopping centre does a wee on the floor where people pass through, and owner quickly mops it up with tissue. Dogs that stop in the streets and refuse to walk on. My towel at the hotel is a large seersucker piece of material. The small towels are linen not towelling. The focaccia bread is so salty but lovely and light with a little oil on one side. The streets teem with people in the morning but shops close at 12 noon and open again at 3 p.m., even the banks. There's hardly a person on the street when I finish my lesson. Same faces at the café each morning. Man with dog is drinking coffee standing at the bar. Bar was packed when I came in and suddenly they've all gone. Someone is delivering toilet rolls and others are singing along with the radio. How was your day? Glad Ella is able to visit. Hope you're feeling stronger. Lots of love from me. N xx

Wednesday 17 June 2015

– Wednesday morning here. We're having good rain at the moment. Great for our gardens. Do you find many Italians you meet have rels in Australia? Love my foreign correspondent reports. Jenny

Wednesday 17 June 2015

– Dear Jenny, great to get the rain. Sometimes the garden is so dry in winter. I watched Julia Gillard and the Labor mob on the ABC podcast which was broadcast last night. What did you think of it? I think from speaking to Paolo's parents that people from the south of Italy came to Australia. Maybe they were poorer down there after the war. Paolo says people from Naples are into everything. When it became compulsory to wear seat belts, they made T-shirts with the belt painted across them so it would appear they were wearing belts! Saw an Italian beggar asleep in siesta time under the eaves of a building in the paws of his sleeping dog. They both beg every day in the same place. Lots of young boys about six years wearing glasses and even younger. The Bangladeshi manager of the hotel wants to come to Australia. I told him to ring the embassy. Someone gave me a counterfeit note, a 20-euro note worth about $28. A lady at a gelato shop told me when I tried to buy a gelato. I don't know whether to try passing it on when I buy something. When I look at it, it seems lighter in weight than the real ones. I thought I'd put it with the real ones in my purse so I won't know when I choose it to pay someone! Is that a bad thing to do? The dogs are barking and the ex-prostitute sisters in the café are clanging the coffee cups this morning. I hope today went well for you. Love, Nerelle

PS Someone is singing while sitting at the bar. Men often sing on buses, in cafés and in the street. I think I'll have to try to speak to local Italians about the story about Italians coming to Australia to live. On the bus yesterday, a strange man started to talk to me in Italian about his bus tickets and bus passes, and when we got off I think he asked me to have a coffee. I declined. No one speaks English where I live. N x

Thursday 18 June 2015

– Dear Jenny, how are you? I hope days are spent happily and you'll be able to sit outside on a sunny day for a short while and enjoy that glass of wine. And yes, I am at the café/bar. It's again hot. We've had a few cool days of rain. I'm over my homesickness for the time being. I know it will return on occasions. Anna is less Soviet and lessons are happy again. She was very kind and arranged train tickets to Verona and a hotel so I can see *Aida* in an open arena on Saturday night. I guess this has been my dream about Italy. There are lots of antique markets in my street today. Thinking of you. With love from Nerelle.

PS My greatest joy each night is watching *Moser* and the original *Commissar Rex* program. However, it's dubbed into Italian and he's *Commissario Rex* here. N x

Thursday 18 June 2015

– I love the way we can tell the other how we feel at the time – but we are allowed to amend and change our views too. Have a great time but I do miss you. Jenny

Sunday 21 June 2015

– Thinking of you, Nerelle, and what you're doing now. Ben took me on trip to Bungendore today. It's growing and we had an interesting time driving on the back road to Collector. Thinking of you always. Jenny

Sunday 21 June 2015

– Dear Jenny, so pleased you enjoyed Bungendore and Collector. You and Ben are becoming huge travellers. Keep enjoying. Love, Nerelle

PS I had a strange hotel experience in Verona. Booked a double room in a hotel and ended up in a single room in someone's house. It was a child's room with all toys in it. No lock on the door. Strange experience but interesting. It was run by a young business woman. I think it was her parents' house.

Monday 22 June 2015

– Dear Jenny, thinking of you too. Back to lessons today. It's my last week here. I've really enjoyed living among Italians. They're nicer than Russians. Hope today was a good one for you. Love, Nerelle

Monday 23 June 2015

– Dear Jenny, hope today was a good one for you. I bet little Lucy is growing fast and is beautiful. In my café – and ladies behind the bar suggested a beer so I'm enjoying one. Love, N

Wednesday 24 June 2015

– Dear Jenny, on another small trip by train half an hour from Genoa. The sea is beautiful but all the beaches are pebbly. N xxx

Friday 26 June 2015

– Hi Jenny, how are you? I hope each day is OK for you. Impressions: young men here have long hair like Elvis but no Brylcreem! They take a shock of hair in their hands and continually put it into place. I go to Russia tomorrow. They use soft plastic bottles for drinks here then crush them. It makes a horrible noise. Love, N

Sunday 28 June 2015

– Dear Jenny, how are you? I'm now in St Petersburg. More when I catch up on sleep. N xx

Sunday 28 June 2015

– Dear Jenny, I think you sent me a reply but no message came. N xx

Sunday 28 June 2015

– What a goose. I can't wait to see you again. Your stories are terrific. I'm OK but not brilliant. Weather here is beautiful. Ben has taken me on a number of Sunday drives, which I really enjoy. Canberra and surrounds have a real beauty. Hope you have a brilliant time in Russia. Miss you and love you. Jenny.

Sunday 28 June 2015

– Dear Jenny, great to receive an update on your condition. I hope you're able to keep positive and enjoy each day. By the way, I managed to pass on the fake $20 Euro at Aida. I bought a blanket there as it was so cold. I passed it on there but the seller knew and treated it the equivalent of $8. At least I got some mileage out of it. This text should say 'from Russia with love'! N x

Monday 29 June 2015

– Dear Jenny, can't sleep. It's almost midnight and someone in the building is renovating and lightly hammering! I've been thinking about Antonia's bedroom where I sleep, and how I and lots of other students have been occupying it for the last eight years. As well as Antonia's clothes in the wardrobe and pictures of family on the walls, this room has traces of my life as well in the things I leave in this room for my next visit, such as the book about St Petersburg that Phil gave me on my first trip here. There are my old Russian dictionary and lesson books as well. Now Antonina has aged and I'm the only student she will accept. After so many years she has reached the point where she doesn't want to worry abut students in her home to care for and worry over any more. Antonina was in hospital with asthma for ten days before my arrival. I can see that she's not as strong as she was and her hearing and memory have faded as well. My teacher Evgueny has told me that his mother at 93 died suddenly last week. And the wild cat Antonina fed for many years, as it visited many people for food, has died as well. Someone blocked up the hole in the side of the building where it went for warmth and it couldn't get out to feed. What a woeful lot of words this turned out to be. Sorry. Love from me. N

Monday 29 June 2015

– There's an article at least to be written about your experience over the years. Do think about it. :-) Jenny

Monday 29 June 2015

– Dear Jenny, will think about the article. Sorry for being so not cheerful. N

Monday 29 June 2015

– I'd give you big hug if I could. Jenny

Monday 29 June 2015

– Dear Jenny, thanks. Hugs from me to you too. Take care and aim for enjoying that glass of wine. N xx

Monday 29 June 2015

– Wine at the Rendezvous restaurant! Jenny

Monday 29 June 2015

– Dear Jenny, that's a date! Nerelle

Tuesday 30 June 2015

– Hello, Jenny. I'm on a break at school. Weather a little colder than Italy. N

Wednesday 1 July 2015

– How many weeks until you come home – no pressure! Love you, Nerelle. Jenny

Wednesday 1 July 2015

– Dear Jenny, arrive home on 19 July. Not long now. How are you doing? Lots of love from me. N xx

Thursday 2 July 2015

– Dear Jenny, I have one small problem which may make you laugh. In the school toilet we can't flush used toilet paper. There are two bins with foot pedals but one is behind the toilet, and opening the other is difficult as it's impeded by pipes. So I'm left with soiled paper accumulating in my hands! What do I do? Wash hands thoroughly with the little soap there is here.

At the ballet last night, a young boy with parents next to me played games on a small iPad. Had to shield my eyes from the glare from the game. People were talking as well.

Have you been getting out much? Love you. N xx

Saturday 4 July 2015

– Dear Jenny, are you OK? You're getting up when I'm going to sleep. N xx

Saturday 4 July 2015

– Hi Nerelle. Am staying at Naomi's while Ben's children are down. Feel OK but not too brilliant. Love to hear from you. You'll have so much to tell me. Love you heaps. Jenny.

Saturday 4 July 2015

– Dear Jenny, so glad to receive your news and to know you're OK. I hope you're able to enjoy each day while watching Lucy grow. Russian observations: Igor, Antonina's son, has just returned from holiday in the country and very excited about bringing back milk which he got from the cow this morning. Won't be pasteurised! Lots of love from me to you. N x

Sunday 5 July 2015

– Dear Jenny, I have to report that the prostitute is still doing business in the apartment across the way from my window in Antonina's building, and since the neighbours called the police when her clients got noisy last night, all is now quiet. N xx

Sunday 5 July 2015

– Hi, Jenny, More impressions to keep you amused. 'Coffee go'. This is a sign for coffee to go – a new fashion in St Petersburg. There are guards in all the shopping centres as usual but this year some are wearing bulletproof vests! N xx

Monday 6 July 2015

– Hi, Nerelle. Can't top your stories but Ben took the children to the National Zoo to stay overnight. He said best thing ever and recommends everyone try it. Evening meal and breakfast were great too. Hope all is going really well. Thinking of you. Jenny :-)

Monday 6 July 2015

– Hi, Jenny, so great to receive your text. Staying overnight is really something! What a great thing to do. I'm sure you're enjoying being with your grandchildren. I hope today has been a good one for you. I'm ready to come home. These last two weeks will go quickly. Lots of love from me to you. N xx

PS Evgueny my teacher was going off to sleep in my class today. He sleeps badly at night. More impressions: milk in Russia can be half water. All seem to know about this. Am in an old coffee shop. Automatic grand piano is playing Christmas songs! N xx

Monday 6 July 2015

– To me it sounds so glamorous and exciting. How do people

feel about the Greek situation? Do you get a chance to hear/ understand local opinion? Glad you'll be home soon. Jenny

Monday 6 July 2015

– Dear Jenny, people interested in the Greeks. They seem to think it will be a good idea to leave the Union. However, they're more interested in Ukraine situation. I bought a mug for Antonina with Putin's face on it. I said to the seller, 'He's a hero?' The young man just shrugged, not in agreement. I think things will get better when the old Soviet generations of Antonina's time and her son's age die. Young people now travel and have broadened their minds. Don't know where this leaves Putin. Russia lives on corruption. Everyone has to pay workers extra just to get ordinary service. This is how the public servants are able to live better than the rest. This is how lowly paid doctors survive. Now people who run universities take money to pass doctors who don't pass their exams, and others who pay to be accepted into university to avoid army service where the boss soldiers are known to shoot and beat young soldiers! What a place to live! N xx

Tuesday 7 July 2015

– Dear Jenny, the main problem for today was how to keep dry on thirty-minute walk to school in the rain. The big pipes take water from buildings and then water flows over the footpath to the road. But how to avoid this water flow? I decided to jump over the water where it flowed from the pipe then I got lost in a detour. I took back streets through markets where clothes manikins were wet and owners stood around in the rain. Man from one of the Stans showed me the way out of the market. All day in wet clothes and wet shoes. Quite cold. Went to a movie made in England but dubbed into Russian. Sat in comfortable seat and had wine during movie while my shoes dried out. That was my day. How's your day? N xx

Wednesday 8 July 2015

– Dear Jenny, would you feel well enough to go to Bangarra Dance on Friday night with someone else? It's on at the Canberra theatre and to see the contemporary Aboriginal dance is wonderful. Phil can't use our tickets. Let me know. Love N xx

Thursday 9 July 2015

– Dear Nerelle, I don't think I could manage, so regretfully I'll have to pass. I'm back home now and it's great, although Naomi and Matt were so good. Big hug to you. Jenny

Thursday 9 July 2015

– Dear Jenny, sorry you're unable to go to Bangarra. Glad you're back home. I imagine you nice and warm by your fire reading. Lots of love from me. N xx

– Dear Jenny, I hope this week has been OK for you. Counting down the days now. Life in Russia – observations: when I was at a play with Antonina and her son's wife Allie, she answered her phone and spoke on it during the play, and Antonina complained loudly she couldn't hear. This week Antonina has given me a beach towel so well used it's now a rag with holes in it. I do have a small one which is OK. Love to you from me. N xx

Friday 10 July 2015

– It makes you think how lucky we are in so many ways. What insights you're gaining. I made salmon cakes from Kate Shelton's book for Ben and me for tea. I was spent after that but glad to have made the effort. Can't wait to see you. Lots of love. Jenny

Friday 10 July 2015

– Dear Jenny, glad you're able to prepare food. I guess eating for you is still difficult but hope you're able to enjoy some food. Ben would have enjoyed the salmon cakes, I'm sure. I guess he misses the children. I took your advice this morning before class and wrote about my room in St Petersburg. Here it is. Nerelle

Portrait of a room

The room is of moderate size and furnished modestly with a narrow bed, a small chest of drawers with television on top, a clothes cupboard, a small fridge and a desk and chairs. There are two flowerpots on the wide window ledge of the huge windows which look out upon a small garden which contains flowers and a memorial to a much-loved family cat Femir, who was the prince of the family for sixteen years. The other view from the window is of other apartment windows and three balconies. One balcony is especially interesting as it is the home of a prostitute who over the years has accumulated and is still accumulating sufficient money for a stable life. After several police call-outs in the past, now there are rare occasions when her clients get drunk and make a lot of noise, and throw bottles from her balcony.

Yes, we are in Russia in the centre of Saint Petersburg and for the last eight years I have occupied this room every summer when I become a student of Russian at a Swiss school in Saint Petersburg. In total I have spent about ten months in this room. Its usual occupant is Antonina, a Russian babushka-grandmother who has worked for the school over many years and has taken in countless numbers of students from all countries of the world. As I re-examine this room, I realise that my traces of occupancy are here with its owner's.

It's the photos on the wall which paint a picture of its owner babushka. Above the bed there are drawings of flowers and country and lake scenes. On the opposite wall are family pictures. They are of her children and grandchildren, and babushka Antonina as a young woman, now in her eighty-third year. Since my first visit, her diabetes has reached another level and she has recently been hospitalised with asthma. Her hearing and memory have diminished. She also economises on the use of the TVs in the house because government directions this year mean that dwellers will pay more for utilities such as electricity and water.

Antonina was a teenager at the time of the Leningrad blockade. Her father died at the front and she and her sister and brother were forced to move towards the east of Russia, where her mother made matches as a factory worker.

After the war, her mother sold her blood to feed her family. After finishing school, Antonina worked in a factory but was encouraged to study nursing at night school. As a nurse, she worked in a factory and then in an orphanage.

The other photos are of her daughter and her three children, and of her son who, at age fifty-nine, lives with Antonina with his wife. Antonina's daughter in early womanhood married a Georgian and bore a son and daughter. Both mothers were dismayed at the marriage and Antonina tells the story of the mother-in-law casting a spell on her daughter, who became very ill until a *Caldoni* (healer) cured her. Her grandson with his dark Georgian looks was saved by the family from the compulsory spell in the army because with his dark colouring he would not have survived. Antonina's daughter is now happily remarried and has another daughter.

Antonia's son was married to an alcoholic and after separation brought a girlfriend from the country to live in the apartment with Antonina. However, Antonina returned home one day to find the girlfriend had changed all the locks and she was locked out of her apartment!

There were times in Antonina's two-bedroom apartment when students occupied her room and Antonina and the cat slept in the same room as her son and new wife. Now Antonina sleeps on a recently acquired divan in the small kitchen when students arrive. But this year and in future years, I am to be the only student she will welcome into her home.

As I look around the room, I note the traces of my occupation of this room. Every year when I return, I can use the treasures I have left behind, like the travel book my partner gave me on the occasion of my first visit. There are also my old homework books and dictionaries and Russian novels, and many other books other students have left behind.

This year, the curtains which were new when I first came to St Petersburg are not so lovingly tied back, and there are fewer plants on the windowsill to care for. The door lock does not work and the wallpaper is peeling off in one place. The bath towel, which is a beach towel showing the Crimea in Soviet times, is worn and thin with several holes. The reading lamp on the table has long gone. However, the light over the bed now has a second globe, missing for all the years I have been sleeping here. The bed linen is worn with holes but there is a new soft cover over the mattress.

Writing about my attachment to this room I also realise that it reflects life in Russia today under the increasing sanctions. Antonia puts up a strong defence of Putin, claiming that Russia itself has all it needs to survive alone. However, her style of life has diminished with the current political circumstances and the loss of students.

Antonina's quality of life has also diminished. Her only sister died two years ago and her friend who lives nearby is housebound through ill health. Her grandchildren have grown up and are busy with their own activities. I realise that my story is about life in its full bloom and in its fading years. Nerelle

Saturday 11 June 2015

– Dear Jenny, not long now until I'm home. It will be just great to come and see you after six weeks. I hope I've kept you amused with my foreign correspondent tales. Lots of love to you from me. N xx

Sunday 12 June 2015

– Dear Nerelle, I'm reading *The Bush* by Don Watson – the book you gave me. It's great, thank you so much. Went to Fyshwick markets yesterday. Bought very little really but it was lovely to get out and see everything again. Why did I think of marketing as a chore? I hope you're enjoying yourself. Time went quickly but I bet you'll be glad to be home to see Phil. Much love to you from me. Jenny

Sunday 12 July 2015

– Dear Jenny, lovely to learn you've been out to the markets. I'm so glad you were able to do that. A pity it's so cold, so I hear. It will be lovely to see you as well as Phil and Annie, your friend the cat. I'm counting off every day now. Weather not good here. Today it will be fifteen degrees and cloudy. N

Sunday 12 July 2015

– Am so glad I rate up with Annie. :-) Jenny

Sunday 12 July 2015

– Dear Jenny, I had an adventure yesterday on a trolley bus. When I got on, the conductor was sleeping. When he awoke, I asked him where a street was. He asked me where I came from. Asked me my age, what I worked as and all sorts of things. He had few teeth and a kind face. He wanted to lunch with me. I got off and on the way home caught his trolleybus again and he insisted on my sitting next to him. Said I was a great person as I did not smoke, take drugs or drink. Asked if I was retired. Insisted on giving me a ticket but wouldn't take any money. This is rare here as conductors are poorly paid and the locals pay for tickets but don't take them so the fare goes to the conductor. Of course all other passengers were interested in our conversation. Anyhow, my heart was lighter for having met him in this environment of unsmiling and rude people. N xx

Sunday 12 July 2015

– Dear Jenny, looked at some Russian Orthodox churches yesterday. At the door there were scarves to cover heads and skirts to cover trousers. I did the head cover but not the skirt. In the first church, two priests were conducting a service. They sang it and wore rich vestments. Very impressive. Next church had many old woman beggars on crutches outside and in this one there were two choirs singing. Fantastic sound of huge voices rising up. I usually light a candle but thought, what's the use, as I don't think there is a God, and people were drinking holy water and genuflecting even before they entered the church. They kiss all the holy icons. On the door of the church was a sign which said, 'No photographs no eating and no lipstick!' How strict is that! I went to a Catholic mass as well, where ladies did not have to wear scarves or skirts. At school we were taught that Catholic masses are the same everywhere in the world. That was true here, although I did get sprayed by the priest with holy water from a big brush as he walked past. I guess the sameness of the mass everywhere can be compared with McDonalds, which is the same worldwide. N xx

Tuesday 14 July 2015

– Hello, Jenny, I'm so excited about the diminishing days here that I forgot to say hello to you today. I hope the day was OK for you. It has been only twelve and fourteen degrees here. And it's raining. Summer not a good one so far. Tonight we're going to a Dostoevsky play called *The Idiot*. I've been translating it in class. Love from me. N xx

Tuesday 14 July 2015

– I know that play and like it! I am so looking forward to seeing you. Jenny

Tuesday 14 July 2015

– Dear Jenny, I just had a funny experience in that café where the automatic piano plays. I think a man asked his Muslim wife to take my photo with him. I asked him the reason and he said I'm very photogenic. I'm having a glass of wine and straight away thought they would not approve but he made sure he placed the glass in the photo. Maybe he'll show those at home the bad Western habits! Lots of love to you from me. N xx

PS Maybe he thought he was having a photo with a typical Russian woman!

Wednesday 15 July 2015

– Dear Jenny, I'm very glad to say that this is almost my last text to you before I leave St Petersburg. I think I'll feel the cold in Canberra although the temperature hasn't been high here. I hope you've been able to get out a little. If you're up to it, you might enjoy a small walk to see Helen's sister-in-law's house at 10 Carrington Street, which will be up for sale soon, as I know how you like to look at houses. I hope today was a good day for you. Lots of love to you from me. N xx

Wednesday 15 July 2015

– So looking forward to seeing you. Would love to do a house sticky beak – but will keep comments to myself. Naomi and Matt got official legal recognition as Lucy's birth parents today. They're so happy. Have a lovely, safe journey home. Love you. Jenny

Wednesday 15 July 2015

– Dear Jenny, looking forward to seeing you too and to chat with you. So happy for Naomi and Matt. Little Lucy will have grown since I saw her. Love you too. N x

Friday 17 July 2015

– Dear Jenny, Looking forward to seeing you soon. I feel very happy as I pack my bags this morning for the return trip. See you soon. Love. Nerelle xxx

Friday 17 July 2015

– Have a great trip home. Can't wait to have a laugh with you. Love. Jenny

Friday 17 July 2015

– Dear Jenny, me too. See you soon. Love. Nerelle

Home again

On Monday 20 July 2015, I spoke to Jenny on the phone. She sounded optimistic and suggested we have coffee at the local coffee shop.

Monday 20 July 2015

– Dear Jenny, will call around at 10.30 a.m. Coffee at Deakin shops or whatever suits you sounds great. Love to see you again. N xx

When I called for Jenny, she was unable to go out for coffee due to her weakened state. She was listening to Radio National on her portable radio and had to get up to switch it off so we could talk. When we parted, she cried about her worry that we would never meet again.

All this time, she has been sleeping on a divan in her living room, unable to use the stairs to her bedroom but not wanting to give into having a bed in the living room. This was soon to change as her children persuaded her to hire a proper bed for better comfort. Friends Ian and Ella would call but would not wake her if she was sleeping.

During the end of July and August, Jenny did not have the strength to enjoy coffee with friends or inspect a property nearby which was for sale, and became progressively weaker, sleeping for a good part of the day.

Late in August, Jenny went to stay at the hospice by the lake. She took the boomerang feather pillow I had bought for her and I was so pleased it was helping to make her more comfortable. She enjoyed using the Jurlique hand cream and slippers I brought to the hospice.

Jenny lived modestly and was always giving little gifts to others to cheer them in times of trauma – me included – and this occurred all throughout our friendship. Before she went to the hospice, she showed me a large framed poster of Australian films hanging on her wall which was to be mine after her death.

The gift of Jurlique hand cream gave Jenny the idea that the forty nurses at the hospice should each receive a small jar of hand cream, as they had to frequently wash their hands. I was commissioned to make it happen. And it did happen, and came the day when she tottered on the arm of Philip and me to the nurses station to present them with the hand cream. On the way, she stopped and hugged my partner, Philip, as if she would never let him go. Jenny was able to visit her garden while she was in the hospice. She took great joy from its beauty.

The texts continued.

Thursday 23 July 2015

– Dear Jenny, I have a very small radio that's good to listen to through ear things. It could be useful if you can't sleep or if you don't want to get up to turn on or off the radio. Would it be useful for you? N xx

Thursday 23 July 2015

– Thanks, Nerelle, but I'm pretty right at present. Hope your body clock is adjusting well. Thanks for your lovely company the other day. Jenny

Thursday 23 July 2015

– Dear Jenny, adjusting slowly but all good. Would you feel like having coffee at Red Hill and look at the view on Saturday or is it better if I just pop in and have a laugh? N xx

Saturday 25 July 2015

Dear Nerelle, I'm feeling really weak and awful in last few days. Can I postpone today until I'm a bit brighter? Thank you. Jenny

Saturday 25 July 2015

– Dear Jenny, of course we can postpone today. I've been thinking of you and thought you weren't feeling too well. I'm here close by. Just text when you feel like company. I'll just sit with you and be with you any time you feel alone. Love you. N xx

> **Saturday 25 July 2015**
>
> – You are the best, Nerelle. Much love to you. Jenny

Monday 27 July 2015

– Dear Jenny, do you feel like a short pop-in visit from me today or would another time be more convenient? N xx

> **Monday 27 July 2015**
>
> – How would Tuesday or Wednesday be for you, Nerelle? That would be lovely. Jenny

Monday 27 July 2015

– Dear Jenny, Wednesday would be good for me. Is morning or afternoon better for you? N xx

> **Monday 27 July 2015**
>
> – Morning would be great.

Monday 27 July 2015

– Dear Jenny, see you Wednesday morning. We'll have a laugh. I hope the doctor's visit goes well. N xx

Friday 31 July 2015

– Dear Jenny, how are you? I was just telling a friend at work how I enjoy visiting you and what lovely company you are. Maybe we can have a look at the house at 10 Carrington Street when it's open for inspection. Don't forget I'm nearby should you like anything. N xx

Friday 31 July 2015

– Love your messages. Love to catch up soon. Maybe we could even manage a coffee shop. I do love you, Nerelle. Jenny

Friday 31 July 2015

– Dear Jenny, just let me know when you feel like a coffee and we'll enjoy it together. Watching *The Bold* because a pipe broke near work and we got an early mark as no water in the toilets. Love you, Jenny. Nerelle xx

Tuesday 4 August 2015

– Dear Jenny, I hope today was OK for you. Helen has invited us to have a look at her house at 10 Carrington Street. I have a good spy book for you. Let me know if you feel like a pop-in visit. N xx

Friday 7 August 2015

– Dear Nerelle, thank you for your messages. I've felt quite sick and very tired in the last week. I hope I can perk up a bit soon. Rachel arrives today, which will be good. You pop in any time. I love seeing you. Jenny

Friday 7 August 2015

– Dear Jenny, I thought you weren't feeling good. I was worried. You're always in my thoughts. Lovely to get your text. Glad Rachel will be with you. Will pop in during the weekend. Love you. Nerelle

Thursday 13 August 2015

– Dear Jenny, lovely to see you brighter yesterday. I hope we didn't tire you. Let me know if you just feel like someone to be with you at any time you're by yourself. No need to talk. Just companions reading or looking at TV together. N xxx

Thursday 20 August 2015

– Dear Jenny, called in yesterday but coincided with nurse's visit. Lucy is lovely. N xx

Friday 21 August 2015

– Hi Jenny, I hope you're doing OK. Popped in at lunch time today but you might have been resting or out. Love from me. N xx

Saturday 22 August 2015

– Dear Jenny, Helen has offered to show us the house in Carrington Street any afternoon except Wednesday if you feel up to it. Love. N

> **Saturday 22 August 2015**
>
> – Dear Nerelle, I'll ring you tomorrow morning if OK with you. Jen

Saturday 22 August 2015

– Dear Jenny, that will be good. Thinking of you. All my love. N

Monday 24 August 2015

– Dear Jenny, thinking of you today. No need to reply. Love. N

> **Tuesday 25 August 2015**
>
> – Thank you, Nerelle. Things get tough sometimes, don't they. So glad you are my friend. Jenny

Tuesday 25 August 2015

– Dear Jenny, you're very brave and a wonderful role model for your friends and family. There is good in your terrible tragedy. It may be that you're bringing your family closer into a strong bond which will last forever and I'm sure there are more wonderful gifts you're giving. For me it's the gift of our long friendship which is surrounded by love. N xx

On Wednesday 26 August 2015, I received a phone call from Jenny from the hospice but she did not leave a message. We spoke a few days later and she was so happy to be there in her 'four-star accommodation'.

Monday 31 August 2015

– Hi Jenny, I'm looking forward to visiting you in your 'four-star accommodation today'. Is lunchtime around 12.30 OK? N xx

Monday 31 August 2015

– Great. Jen

Thursday 3 September 2015

– What an amazing lady you are. How did I get you for such a friend. Love you heaps. Jenny

Thursday 3 September 2015

– Dear Jenny, I'm so pleased you're settled by the lake with such professional help and are enjoying being there. So many want to visit you. They must think you're a popular lady at the hospice and you are. You have always thought about your friends and what would make them happy. And you're receiving back the lovely thoughts and deeds you gave. Have a good rest. So pleased you're tramping around the corridors there and enjoying your food. You're wonderful and brave. I think of you all the time and send you all my love. Just ask for anything you may think of. Enjoy TV and sleep well. N xx

Thursday 3 September 2015

– Again, here's looking at you kid. Jenny

Friday 4 September 2015

– Dear Jenny, have a lovely relaxing day. N xx

Saturday 5 September 2015

– Jurlique hand cream is beautiful. Thank you, my lovely friend. Jenny

Saturday 5 September 2015

– Dear Jenny, glad you like that brand. Did you have a trip home today? *Halifax* is on TV tonight. N xx

Sunday 6 September 2015

– Dear Jenny, just sending you hello. N xx

Monday 7 September 2015

– Dear Jenny, a progress report for you. A few things for you to think about regarding the hand cream for forty nurses at the hospice. One option via the internet would be 50ml tubes of Mog Marshmallow hand cream for $11 each. It would cost $440 plus. Have a think about it. Kacey at work has also offered to do some searches. She suggested buying the jars. She has bought sun cream in bulk for the office but paid $12 for each and thinks it's difficult to find less expensive alternatives. N xx

Wednesday 9 September 2015

– Dear Jenny, the 40x50g plastic jars arrive next Tuesday. Cost was $37.80 plus post of $18.50. I bought sufficient Dr Lewinn's hand and nail cream for $119.70. Wicker basket with handle $14.99 and cellophane $2.99. Total is $193.98. Don't worry about payment now. We'll see if I have enough cream. In all, there's 2,250 grams, which should fill 40x50 gram jars with a bit left over. Phil is doing the labels tomorrow so we're hot to trot! N xxx

Friday 11 September 2015

– Dear Jenny, I hope today has been enjoyable. Are you lining up for *Midsomer Murders* tonight on the TV? N xx

Saturday 12 September 2015

– Hi Jenny, when is the best time, today or tomorrow, to visit? N xx

Saturday 12 September 2015

– Tomorrow would be great! Jen

Saturday 12 September 2015

– Dear Jenny, see you then. Is there a good time you prefer? Nerelle

Saturday 12 September 2015

– About 10 a.m.? Jen

Saturday 12 September 2015

– Dear Jenny, see you then. N

Monday 14 September 2015

– Dear Jenny, thinking of you and hope today is a better one to enjoy N xx

Monday 14 September 2015

– Dear Jenny, exciting developments with Malcolm Turnbull. Bad for the Labor Party. N xx

> **Monday 14 September 2015**
>
> – Where is Margy? [Ex PM Tony Abbott's wife.] Jen

Monday 14 September 2015

– At the hairdressers! Nerelle

> **Monday 14 September 2015**
>
> – Yeh! Jen

Monday 14 September 2015

– Dear Jenny, it will be great TV tonight. Although I was looking forward to the *Four Corners* report about ISIS. N xx

> **Monday 14 September 2015**
>
> – Don't forget Radio National and Philip Adams. Jen

Monday 14 September 2015

– Dear Jenny, they're a must-listen, I think. I go to sleep too late because of Philip Adams. N xx

> **Monday 14 September 2015**
>
> – I love YOU. Jen

Monday 14 September 2015

– Dear Jenny, love you too. Enjoy the political show tonight. N xx

Monday 14 September 2015

– Dear Jenny, received your card today. It's lovely. Thank you for sending it. N xx

Tuesday 15 September 2015

– Talk about where's Wally. MARGY is missing in action. Jenny

Tuesday 15 September 2015

– Dear Jenny, maybe the rumours were true that they were separating when he became PM. I feel a bit sorry for him but I'm so glad he's gone. Friend sent a made-up photo of Julia Gillard standing behind Tony making his speech holding up a card on which was written RYOK? N xx

Tuesday 15 September 2015

– You are a sweetie. Jen

Friday 18 September 2015

– Hi Jenny, I hope that microwave door for the hotties is behaving. The jars have arrived and production will begin tomorrow. N xx

Friday 18 September 2015

– Thanks, N. Tomorrow is perfect. [Pain management was having an effect on Jenny by this time.]

Friday 18 September 2015

– Dear Jenny, hope you're having a good day. N

Sunday 20 September 2015

– Dear Jenny, the last edition of *Halifax* is on the ABC now. N xx

Monday 21 September 2015

– Dear Jenny, lovely to see you this afternoon. Please let me know if I can help Ben with the red jumper. Sleep well. As always, lots of love from me to you. Nerelle xx

Wednesday 23 September 2015

– Dear Jenny, sending you all my love. Nerelle xx

On Thursday 24 September 2015, Jenny requested daffodils to be placed in her room and I left them at the hospice then received a note from her sister that she wanted to see me. Jenny also wanted Phil and me to visit on Friday to have champagne. On Friday, she was sitting up in the chair waiting for us at 5 p.m. as arranged. She sat close to us and chatted. No champagne. Jenny a bit fuzzy. The nurse put her back in bed as we could not manage to do it as she was so weak. We chatted more and Phil heated the bean bags (hotties) and we tucked her into bed and said goodnight.

Jenny was awaiting the arrival of her daughter Rachel, husband Duncan and grandchildren from Western Australia. She had already planned the things at the hospice she would show the children. She wanted me to be present during her home visit the next day but I felt it was important for her to spend the whole time with her family. I worried over my decision all day.

On Saturday 26 September 2015, Jenny visited her house in the morning, walked a little in the corridor of the hospice, and her family visited. Her sister was the last one to see her before she died. Jenny told her sister she wanted to turn to the wall, listen to Radio National and have a sleep. Jenny died during that night. She had never wanted people to sit by her bed while she rested, much to her sister's disappointment that she could have been present when Jenny died.

It always seemed to me that Jenny was resigned to her fate from the outset and showed bravery when she decided that the chemotherapy was too harsh for her denuded body. She then decided not to continue with any type of treatment. I know, however, she experienced times of terrible disappointment and sadness about her illness and what it would bring.

Jenny's last words to me were 'Please don't forget me.'

Her family carried out her wishes about her funeral. Jenny had stuck to her convictions and remained a non-believer. She left instructions for all to wear a flower at her farewell and we each received a flower on arrival at the undertaker's premises. Her coffin was covered in spring flowers. And do you know, the males with whom we had worked forty-one years ago in the Property Directorate were all there. Her family and friends spoke about her life and she had left instructions that I was to speak as well.

I had written some notes but they were too small to see through my tears. However, I was able to say, 'Through her illness Jenny reached her highest self. She gave and received love with a loving heart. Her gift to her family was and is the profound and loving experience of caring for their mother and sister. Jenny was such a kind person, always thoughtfully giving gifts of flowers in support of a friend. Our friendship, which began through work, was full of laughter and enjoyment of being able to pop in to visit on a whim. We walked through life together for forty-one years and I thought we would be walking into old age together. I was privileged to be Jenny's friend.'

Afterwards, we drank champagne in a lovely garden Jenny had chosen, with birds singing in the trees. The day was perfect. Jenny arranged for all to take home a potted flower plant.

A few days later, Phil and I and her family farewelled her spirit with a champagne toast in her garden which she loved so much. Little Lucy was there to farewell her grandmother.

A little while later, her house was auctioned and a new owner would move in. In the meantime, Jenny's daughter Naomi asked me if I would water Jenny's garden while she was away. I did so until the new owner took over occupancy. Unexpectedly, this bi-weekly watering helped me to rationalise the events of the last six moths. As I watered Jenny's lovely garden, I came to realise how she lovingly planted her garden in which she had so much pride, introducing mysterious corners and little animal ornaments throughout for the wonder of her grandchildren. I then started to re-establish and nurture my own garden and that has helped my grieving for Jenny.

Jenny's photo is on my mantelpiece, her bequest is in my bedroom and the African violet she gave me many years ago has bloomed for me for three months of this year. As I prepare to return to Russia and Italy this year, my thoughts are with my 'travelling companion' of last year and I think I will never have such a friend in all my lifetime.

www.ingramcontent.com/pod-product-compliance
Lightning Source LLC
Chambersburg PA
CBHW030917080526
44589CB00010B/346